My Side Income

7 ways to put more money in your pocket

Sonel Soulouque

My Side Income:
7 ways to put more money in your pocket

Copyright © 2018 Sonel Soulouque
Registered with the United States Copyright Office, Washington, D.C. All rights reserved. No part of this book may be reproduced in any form without the author's consent.
Cover design by Hans Clough, HansClough.com
Back cover photograph of Sonel Soulouque by Jennifer Martin-Melgarejo
Image credits:
Travel picture by fcl1971 from freeimages.com
ESL instruction picture by Dan McDonald from freeimages.com
Investment picture by Thomas Picard from freeimages.com
Lyft car picture by Maaillustrations from freeimages.com
Tutoring picture by Gonzalo Silva from freeimages.com
ATM machine picture by Vaughan Willis from freeimages.com
Travel picture by Maaillustrations from freeimages.com
Section images:
freeqration.com/image/writing-paper-pen-hands-people-business-232705
freeqration.com/image/woman-person-people-desk-work-business-photos-2064806
freeqration.com/image/watch-business-suit-man-close-up-indoors-photo-2064355
freeqration.com/image/rain-human-hand-drops-selective-focus-1626130

To my parents who,

by the grace of God,

made me who I am today.

My Side Income: 7 ways to put more money in your pocket

Table of Contents

Perspective..9

A Word from the Author..11

    Notes..12

Section One: Offline Side Income..13

Tutoring...14

    Introduction...14

    Skills, training, or licensing needed................................15

    How to start (process, time, cost)....................................16

    How to get customers...18

    How to operate...19

    Earning potential..20

    Other benefits...20

    Drawbacks..20

    "What if I don't like it; how do I get out?"....................21

    Summary...21

    Resources for further study...21

    Notes..24

Section Two: Online Side Income..25

Travel Website..26

    Introduction...26

Skills, training, or licensing needed..................28

How to start (process, time, cost)....................29

How to get customers..................................33

How to operate..34

Earning potential.....................................35

Other benefits..38

Drawbacks...38

"What if I don't like it; how do I get out?".........39

Summary...40

Resources for further study...........................40

Notes...42

Section Three: Micro-entrepreneurship Income..........43

Lyft Driving..44

Introduction..44

Skills, training, or licensing needed.................45

How to start (process, time, cost)....................46

How to get customers..................................46

How to operate..47

Earning potential.....................................48

Other benefits..49

Drawbacks...50

"What if I don't like it; how do I get out?".........52

My Side Income: 7 ways to put more money in your pocket

    Summary..52

    Resources for further study.................................52

Tax Preparation..55

    Introduction..55

    Skills, training, or licensing needed....................56

    How to start (process, time, cost).......................57

    How to get customers..59

    How to operate..60

    Earning potential...61

    Other benefits..61

    Drawbacks...62

    "What if I don't like it; how do I get out?"......63

    Summary..63

    Resources for further study.................................64

ESL Instruction..66

    Introduction..66

    Skills, training, or licensing needed....................67

    How to start (process, time, cost).......................68

    How to get customers..69

    How to operate..70

    Earning potential...70

    Other benefits..70

Drawbacks..71

  "What if I don't like it; how do I get out?"....................71

  Summary..72

  Resources for further study...72

ATM Deployment..74

  Introduction..74

  Skills, training, or licensing needed............................76

  How to start (process, time, cost)..............................77

  How to get customers...80

  How to operate..80

  Earning potential..82

  Other benefits...83

  Drawbacks..84

  "What if I don't like it; how do I get out?"....................86

  Summary..86

  Resources for further study...86

  Notes..88

Section Four: Passive Income..89

Investment..90

  Introduction..90

  Skills, training, or licensing needed............................91

  How to start (process, time, cost)..............................91

7

How to find investments...92

Another type of investment..97

How to operate...98

Earning potential...100

Other benefits..101

Drawbacks...101

"What if I don't like it; how do I get out?"..................102

Summary..103

Resources for further study..103

Notes..106

Conclusion...107

Acknowledgments..108

Perspective

"A simple fact that is hard to learn is that the time to save money is when you have some." ~Joe Moore (brainyquote.com)

"Bills never sleep."

When a friend of mine said that, I thought, *How true!*

Month after month, bills for cable or satellite TV, housing, cell phone, internet service, credit cards, car loans, tuition, insurance and so on show up in the mailbox or the inbox. (See pew-socialtrends.org/2007/02/07/what-americans-pay-for-and-how/) Mix in regular expenses like groceries, and most Americans are living paycheck to paycheck—barely staving off late fees, delinquencies, even disconnected services (cable, electricity, internet, water). We pay our bills, and then we're broke until the next paycheck.

What happens when there's an emergency? What happens when the car breaks down, the plumbing fails, or there's a death in the family? What happens when you go into work on Monday morning and discover you no longer have a job?

Most people don't have the recommended three to six months worth of income in a savings account dedicated for just such emergencies.

How do you escape living paycheck to paycheck? For most of us, the answer is simple: more money. But how? Raises and promotions are hard to come by, and most people don't have the option of working overtime for pay every time they need some extra cash.

The good news is this. If you live in America or a similar country, you aren't limited to what your job provides. With a little initiative and hard work, you can go out and create your own opportunities. Creative and talented people (that's you) who want to be financially successful, have many options to put money in your pocket.

Chris Guillebeau got it right when he said, "In today's environment where the idea of a business having any sense of loyalty to its workers has all but disappeared, the side hustle is the new job security." (Chris Guillebeau, *Side Hustle: From Idea to Income in 27 Days*, 2017)

You can escape the gravitational pull of paycheck-to-paycheck living. This book will show you how.

A Word from the Author

Even though I earn a respectable salary as a high school teacher with a master's degree and fourteen years of experience, I am determined not to rely solely on my biweekly paycheck. For one, I don't want to be confined by my salary. I have the ability to earn more, and I'm not waiting around for a raise in order to earn more. Instead, I became a micro-entrepreneur. On March 6, 2018, I won 2nd Runner Up in the Fix Your Business contest from Small Biz sponsored by America's # 1 Small Business Expert, Melinda Emerson.

For many people, the worst thing that could happen to them is losing their job. But, with the right skills, you can adapt and thrive in any situation.

I want to teach you how to adapt and thrive. I want to teach you how break free from the shackles of what someone else thinks you should earn.

In this book, I'll show you what I've done. But this book is about you, not me. I want to share my experiences with you so you can replicate my trajectory or create your own. If you are an entrepreneurial-minded person, you will find great ideas in this book that will steadily put money in your pocket and add to your wealth.

Sonel Soulouque

Notes

Section One: Offline Side Income

Tutoring

"The beautiful thing about learning is that no one can take it away from you." ~B.B. King (values.com)

Introduction

The worldwide tutoring industry is huge. James Marshall Crotty reports, "Market research firm Global Industry Analysts, Inc. (GIA) has released a study this past week stating that the global private tutoring market is projected to surpass $102.8 billion by 2018. According to GIA, the burgeoning private tutoring market is being driven by the failure of standard education systems to cater to the unique needs of students, combined with growing parental desire to secure the best possible education for their children in a highly competitive global economy." (James Marshall Crotty, "Global Private Tutoring Market Will Surpass $102.8 Billion By 2018," forbes.com/sites/jamesmarshall-crotty/2012/10/30/global-private-tutoring-market-will-surpass-102-billion-by-2018/#1b8d84c82ee0)

While Asia and Europe have are well known for their strong emphasis on tutoring, the demand is also strong here in the United States. The number of private tutoring businesses here in United States is soaring. For example, Kumon has set up more than 1,400 of its Math and Reading Centers across the country. (theweek.com/articles/481041/americas-tutor-boom-by-numbers).

According to earnmydegree.com, "there were 983,000 tutors in the United States in 2014 and that number is expected to grow by 5 to 8% from 2014 through 2024."

Crotty adds, "According to Rebecca Fochek, the Omaha-based founder of Academic Coaching Academy, private in-home tutoring offers an innovative, highly personalized, and secure learning environment for today's stressed and distracted students, who are under increasing pressure to perform well in competitive entrance examinations for leading universities and colleges." (forbes.com)

I was tutored as a college student. And I, in turn, began tutoring others. I've tutored English as a Second Language (ESL) students at a community college. In addition, since becoming a certified teacher of high school French, I tutor students in French after school and over the summer.

If you enjoy teaching others, tutoring is a great opportunity to earn extra income on the side.

Skills, training, or licensing needed

While it helps to have experience and/or licensing as a professional teacher, those qualifications are not necessary for tutoring. You just need to have a solid grasp of your subject area, and the patience to help someone through the steps of understanding it.

Depending on your state and local laws, you may need to register as a sole proprietor or, if you plan to set up a different kind of business entity such as a limited liability company or a partnership, you may need to complete an application or registration process. You may also need to obtain a federal and state employer tax ID number. (care.com)

How to start (process, time, cost)

When starting any new business, especially if you have never been in business or self employed before, you really want to get good advice from mentors who understand the world of business. The SCORE Association (previously known as the Service Corps of Retired Executives) is a 501(c)(3) nonprofit organization that provides free business mentoring services to entrepreneurs in the United States. Learn more at score.org.

You'll need to start by deciding what type of tutor you're going to be. Not sure? A list of categories or specialties is available at lovetoknow.com. Specialties are categorized by age/grade, subject, and other factors such as high-stakes exam preparation. You'll need to decide not only the subject area, but also the level of expertise (grade level or skill level), and age range.

You'll also need to decide how much you will charge. Most tutors charge by the hour. Care.com/tutors will help you get an idea of what other tutors are charging for their services. Charge enough money for your services. Remember, as a self employed person, you are paying all your own business expenses as well as the employer's half of Social Security. You receive no sick leave or other benefits. So these things need to be factored into your price. In addition, people tend to undervalue tutors and other professionals who charge too little. On the other hand, you don't want to price yourself out of the market. Study the market, and price accordingly. You'll also want to establish a cancellation and no-show policy.

Determine where you are going to meet your students. I usually meet my students at the local public library. Some people provide tutoring services online via Skype or other delivery systems. One source provided this helpful bit of information: "Online learning now depends more on the ability of educators and trainers to tutor and support learners online than on the technology itself." (Dr. Ian Heywood, 2000 World Open Learning Conference and Exhibition, Birmingham, England lsche.net/old/resources/online/ol_quotes.htm)

Make sure you know what materials you will bring into the tutoring environment, and clarify what you expect your student to bring. (books, workbooks, paper, pencil/pen, laptop, timer)

Prepare your marketing materials. (fliers, postcards, business cards, online ads, blog posts, social media posts)

If you want to go big and set up a tutoring service where you hire tutors and attract dozens or hundreds of students, you might want to consider purchasing a tutoring business franchise. It will cost more, of course, than just setting up shop as a one-man/one-woman operation. A recent web search put start up costs if you want to purchase a Kumon Center franchise in the $6,000 to $9,000 range. Other choices are also available. You'll want to do your research and determine what's best for you.

You can find additional information and resources on how to start you tutoring service by visiting cleverapple.com. This site provides a wealth of resources including start up, training, marketing strategies, online tutoring.

How to get customers

I began by creating fliers and placing them in various locations throughout the city where I have lived for years. People who want to learn French see these fliers, and every so often I get a call from a new potential student. That approach has worked great for me, and I believe it can work for you.

In addition to the one-on-one tutoring that you can provide at a local library, at your home, at the home of your student, or elsewhere, you can also set up online tutoring or distance tutoring. Here's how: Post your tutoring initiative online on social media such as Facebook to attract students worldwide. You can also start a blog in your area of expertise, and let people know at the end of each post that you are available for tutoring. Be sure to explain what a potential student needs to do if they are interested.

It's good to give prospects more than one contact option. Some people like to make phone calls; some don't. Some like to email; some don't. Some may want to know prices before they talk to you. I'm not saying you need to include all that information; just know that you might lose a few prospects if you don't.

Another way to obtain students is to register with a tutoring service like Wyzant, preply.com, tutor.com, tutapoint.com, etutrorworld.com, mindlaunch.com, webwisetutors.com, and so on. Each of these companies is structured a little differently than the others. For example, when you register with Wyzant, your students will be local, and lessons will be delivered in person. Wyzant collects the money from the student and then pays you. Preply.com allows you to set your own price for your tutoring service and to connect with students via Skype.

How to operate

When tutoring, you'll want to take into account your student's needs. Each student will be at a different place in his or her understanding of the subject matter. Your role is to build a strong relationship, to meet your student where he or she is at (in terms of their understanding), and help them take the next step in learning. There are many resources online that will help you structure your tutoring sessions. (For example, wikihow.com/Be-a-Good-Tutor)

You'll want to agree ahead of time on when and how payment will be collected. Will you expect cash at the end of the tutoring session? Do you accept credit cards or PayPal? Will you charge weekly, monthly, hourly? Ideally, you'll want to work out those arrangements before you meet for the first time, or early on in that first meeting.

Earning potential

When I was a college student tutoring ESL students at that community college, I was paid $7 per hour. Obviously, that was a very low rate.

According to PayScale.com, "A Tutor earns an average wage of $17.28 per hour. Skills that are associated with high pay for this job are Physics, French Language, Math, Science, and Reading."

Care.com/tutors lists the average tutoring rate at $14.00 per hour. Care.com/tutoring-jobs will give you an idea of what the market is currently expecting to pay. The website also connects service providers with customers in the areas of child care, senior care, pet care and housekeeping.

Other benefits

There is a real satisfaction that comes from helping others learn. In many ways, tutoring is its own reward. You've been given knowledge that you pass on to another person. It's a way of leaving a legacy to those who follow behind you.

Drawbacks

Will you get rich tutoring? Probably not, unless you build a business that hires hundreds of tutors and attracts thousands of students. For 99% of tutors, it's a respectable and relatively easy way to make a few extra dollars.

Like any other business where you meet with clients, you will find that some people cancel at the last minute, and some people don't show at all. If you don't have a clear cancellation policy, you may find yourself wasting time for zero pay.

"What if I don't like it; how do I get out?"

As with any other business, you need to keep the promises you make. If you've promised to tutor someone for eleven weeks, you need to tutor for eleven weeks barring some catastrophic change in your circumstances like an unexpected and extended hospitalization. But beyond that, this is an easy entry, easy exit business. If you don't like tutoring, you simply stop taking new clients and give your existing clients a reasonable notice.

If you've signed up with a tutoring service, then, of course, you'll need to read your contract carefully to see what, if any, requirements you need to fulfill in order to step away.

Summary

Private tutoring is always in demand. Children, adolescents, and adults all are looking for ways to expand their knowledge and sharpen their skills. By making time available to tutor others in the area(s) of your expertise, you can create a stream of income that can help you eliminate debt, enjoy a new car or a vacation, pay some bills, or build up a nest egg.

Resources for further study

Growth and extent of the global tutoring market:

- forbes.com/sites/jamesmarshallcrotty/2012/10/30/global-private-tutoring-market-will-surpass-102-billion-by-2018/#1b8d84c82ee0
- theweek.com/articles/481041/americas-tutor-boom-by-numbers
- earnmydegree.com

Setting up a business entity:

- care.com

Free mentoring for business start up:

- score.org

Tutor categories

- lovetoknow.com

Online learning quotes

- lsche.net/old/resources/online/ol_quotes.htm

Information on starting and operating a tutoring service:

- cleverapple.com

Tutoring sites and services that connect you with students and/or provide information on tutoring fees/rates:

- wyzant.com
- preply.com
- tutor.com
- tutapoint.com
- etutrorworld.com

- mindlaunch.com
- webwisetutors.com
- care.com/tutors and care.com/tutoring-jobs

How to structure a tutoring session:

- wikihow.com/Be-a-Good-Tutor

What tutors are paid:

- payscale.com
- care.com/tutoring-jobs

Notes

Section Two: Online Side Income

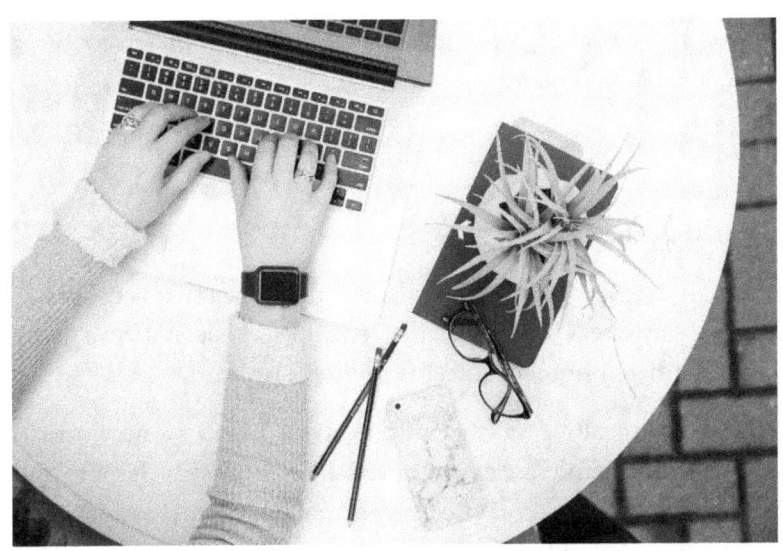

Travel Website

"We travel, some of us forever, to seek other states, other lives, other souls." ~Anais Nin (brainyquote.com)

Introduction

I am an avid traveler. I love visiting new places. I sleep better when I am away overseas. For example, I sleep like a baby when I am at a hotel or a resort in the Caribbean.

And I'm not alone. Everybody needs a break from work to spend some time away by themselves or with family and friends. According to IATA, "on average, every day more than 8 million people fly. In 2013 total passenger numbers were 3.1 billion—surpassing the 3 billion mark for the first time ever." (iata.org/pressroom/pr/Pages/2013-12-30-01.aspx)

US Travel reports that the "direct spending by resident and international travelers in the U.S. averaged $2.7 billion a day, $113.1 million an hour, $1.9 million a minute and $31,400 a second." (ustravel.org/answersheet)

In short, the travel industry is a huge market that any entrepreneur can benefit from—if you have patience and passion for traveling. Today, many people do not visit a travel agency to buy tickets, book hotels, or put together a travel package. Instead, they go online to search for the best travel deals. Rather than fight that trend, I came up with the idea to create my own travel website. And instead of trying to raise millions of dollars to create a custom service to compete with Priceline, Kayak, or other major travel sites, I decided to create an affiliate site. When someone uses my site, they are actually using a major travel site in the background, and I'm paid a commission for bringing the customer to that site.

The idea here is to spend the least to gain the most. I'm on a mission to make money and save money.

Skills, training, or licensing needed

The fundamental skills that you need to run a travel website are:

- basic computer skills
- customer service skills
- financial responsibility
- patience and perseverance.

Do you need a license to become a travel agent?

It depends. In New Jersey, where I live, the current answer is no. No licensing is required. This makes New Jersey an attractive state for people who want to make extra money as a travel agency entrepreneur building an online travel website.

Some states do require licensing, however. The last time I checked, California, Florida, Hawaii, Illinois, Iowa, Louisiana, Massachusetts, Michigan, Nevada, New York, Pennsylvania, Virginia, and Washington all required licensing. (travellaw.com/page/travel-law-faq) You'll want to check with a business attorney in your area to identify any legal or regulatory requirements you'll need to follow when starting your travel agent business.

How to start (process, time, cost)

Starting a travel agency website can cost anywhere from a few hundred dollars to nearly $10,000 or more. (hometravelagency.com/startup-costs) I'll show you how I did it for a minimal investment. When you operate a part-time business as an entrepreneur, you want to find ways to minimize your start up and operating costs, so your revenue comes back into your pocket instead of paying for setting up your business. The best way to do that as a travel agent is to set up an affiliate site. I'll explain how I did that in the next few paragraphs.

To launch a travel website, you'll need two important things: (1) a name for your site, (2) a hosting company.

Your name defines your business, so take your time looking for a name. You might want to Google "how to come up with a business name." After thinking and researching days and nights, I came up with a name that was original, catchy and appealing to the public: "Stopnfly."

Remember, your business will be online, so you need a domain name that matches your business name. Many great domain names are already taken, but with some creativity, you'll find a great name that's still available. In my case, stopnfly.com was available, so I purchased it. When you Google "how to search for a domain name," you'll find a number of sites including godaddy.com who can help you find and register an available domain name. The cost of registering (owning) a domain name is minimal, usually under $20 per year. There are many reliable domain registration companies out there including GoDaddy, Pair Domains, and many others. A quick Google search will help you find the domain registration company that's right for you. I bought my domain through Hostgator. I pay $15 per year for my domain name.

You'll need your travel website hosted on the internet. That means you need a hosting company. Unless you're going to get hundreds, thousands, or more customers a day, a shared hosting plan will probably work fine for you. You might want to Google "best hosting companies," to find a hosting company that will work for you. I found a cheaper host. This host offered a website builder (allowing me to build my site on my own without paying for a website consultant) and a c-panel (so I could control my site myself). I selected Hostgator because they were affordable, and because they offered me a platform that empowered me to build my website without needing technical web development skills. I pay $5.95 per month for my hosting service. Update: In January 2018, I changed my hosting company to Namecheap. Now I only pay $9.98 for an entire year!

Your next step is to find an affiliate service. An affiliate service allows you to place content (text, photos, search bars, and more) on your site which will connect your site with an online travel service like Priceline, Kayak, or whatever. Every time your customer makes a purchase, you are paid a commission, and the online travel service takes care of processing your customer's credit card, issuing the reservations and the electronic tickets, and processing everything else connected with the sale.

Your travel site can provide more than just airline tickets. My site is set up to allow customers to purchase airline tickets, book hotel reservations, make car rental reservations, and purchase travel-related products. Again, all of these transactions are handled by my affiliate services, so they don't require any time or effort on my part.

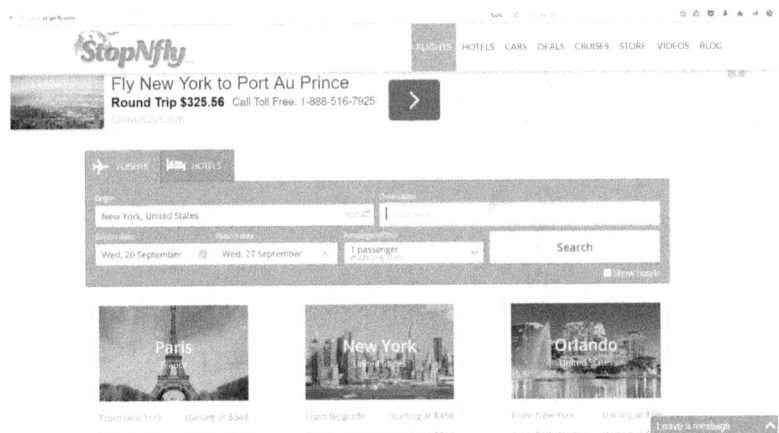

I started with Linkshare/Rakuten[1] as my affiliate provider. All my visitors were transferred to bookingbuddy.com, and Linkshare/Rakuten paid me my commissions. Every time someone visited my site, clicked through and booked a ticket from bookingbuddy, Linkshare/Rakuten paid me a commission. The more tickets people bought through my travel site, the more commission I received into my checking account.

Later, however, I switched to travelerrr.com as my affiliate provider. Now people are transferred to jetradar.com for flights, to hotellook.com for hotels, and to cars.cartrawler.com for car rentals via the search bar at the top of my site. My travel accessories store is linked to Amazon. Update: I just recently

---

1 "Rakuten LinkShare is an affiliate marketing service provider. The company claims it is the largest pay-for-performance affiliate marketing network on the Internet. LinkShare was founded in 1996 by Stephen Messer and Heidi Messer and is headquartered in New York City, with offices in San Francisco, Chicago, Tampa, Tokyo and London. In 2005, Rakuten acquired LinkShare for US $425 million in cash, making LinkShare a wholly owned U.S. division of Rakuten, Inc., a Japanese shopping portal." Rakuten LinkShare was re-branded to Rakuten Affiliate Network in 2014." (en.wikipedia.org/wiki/Rakuten_Linkshare)

switched affiliate providers to Travelpayouts (www.travelpayouts.com), as they provide better commissions.

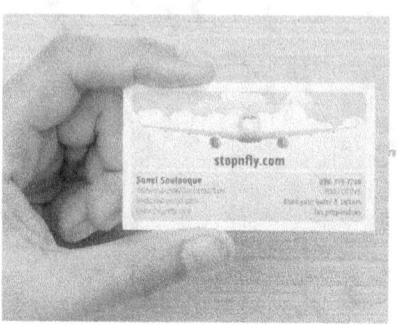

In the beginning, I built my site using a site builder available from my host, Hostgator. Now I no longer use Hostgator's site builder because, travelerrr.com helps with website creation and design, and much more. Visit www.travelerrr.com and scroll down the page for plans and pricing.

I also set up my website with Google AdSense. Google places travel-related ads on my site. Here's how it works: "To make it as basic as possible, you sign up for an AdSense account and add the code to your blog or website. You can choose how your ads look, where they show up, and even what kind of ads you'll accept." (nutsandboltsmedia.com/how-does-adsense-work) Every time someone visits my site and clicks on the ad, Google pays me. That is what's called *pay per click*. The more visitors you get to your site, the more money you will generate into your account. This is called passive income.

While AdSense is free to join and a great source of monetization for your travel website, you do need to be careful how you use it. For example, you cannot get someone to just visit your site to click on ads so you can make money. Google has algorithms to detect fraudulent activity, and will shut down your account if they suspect such activity.

How to get customers

My travel site quickly populated in major search engines like Google, Bing, and Yahoo. Through the cpanel, I have been able to track my visitors to the site. I was amazed to see people in India and China were visiting Stopnfly.com for tickets.

But I didn't just rely on search engines to bring customers to me. I went out and looked for customers. I printed fliers in English and Spanish as well as business cards and placed them anywhere I could in my community and surrounding communities. People saw my fliers, and started calling me for tickets.

How to operate

The website, of course, once set up, operates itself. You don't need to do anything other than help any customers who are having trouble using the website. Once your affiliate links and your Google AdSense is set up, you don't need to do anything more to operate it, other than to continually look for ways to improve your website.

And, while you don't need to take on local customers, I recommend you do, because that's where I make most of my money. I always try my best to look for the best price for my local customers in order to keep them as happy customers, satisfied with the service I provide. Most of the time, I use my own debit card to book the tickets for these customers who call me. I collect the fee from them in cash. Of course, I deposit that cash in my checking account to cover the transaction. In addition, I collect a $25-$30 service fee from these customers to cover my expenses and make a profit on each transaction.

You can put any amount of time into this business that you want. If you advertise locally, your time commitment will depend on the number of customers who contact you for full-service travel assistance. You will want to make sure that your website is hosted by a reliable hosting company that keeps your site online 24/7. You'll want your own internet connection up at all times, so you're able to promptly respond to anyone who contacts you via your website.

Earning potential

According to Gifted Travel Network, there are 2 major sources of revenue for self-employed travel agents:

1) Commission

"When a travel agent makes a booking on behalf of his or her client, most suppliers will pay a commission to the agency. The commission won't be paid until AFTER travel is completed, although some cruise lines now pay commission after final payment is made. As a general practice, the following pay commissions: hotels and hotel chains, cruise lines, tour operators, car rental companies, travel insurance providers, airport transfer companies, shore excursion companies, tour guides and some European rail lines. What's missing? Airlines. The airlines stopped paying travel agency commissions in early 2000's."

2) Service Fees

"The subject of service fees can often be controversial thanks to many "old school" travel agents feeling the heat of competition following the onslaught of online booking engines. Back in the early 1990's travel agencies hardly ever charged service fees … because they didn't have to. But when the airlines eliminated commissions on all international and domestic air, thousands of travel agencies took a huge hit to their bottom lines, so severe that many went out of business. Commission on air often made up 50–70% of an agency's revenue.

Not all travel agents charge service fees, but it is becoming more and more common. Service fees can range drastically. Airline tickets often carry a service fee of $25–$50 per ticket. Full itinerary design can range from $75–$500. Charging a service fee is more of an art than a science and some agents will charge per hour or per person." (giftedtravelnetwork.com/much-travel-agents-get-paid/)

Because travel prices are now so competitive, your commission on each ticket sold through your affiliate program will not be that high—often $1, $2, or $3. On sales to visitors at your website, you make your money by getting high traffic to your site and by offering many options (airline, hotel, car, cruise, travel accessories, Google ads).

You can make much more money with local customers. I charge a $25–$30 service fee for each transaction.

You can make a passive income through Google Adsense. The amount you are paid for each click through varies with the advertiser. For example, one advertiser might pay you $0.10 for a click through. Another might pay you $0.84. Google will pay you when your account reaches a threshold of $100. Understand that your site will need a great deal of traffic before you start making any kind of decent money through Google AdSense. Some website owners earn only a few pennies per month with Google AdSense.

As with any business, you must keep a written record of your income and expenses for tax purposes. If you operate your business as a sole proprietor (as opposed to a partnership or a corporation), you'll need to file a Schedule C with your individual income tax return (1040) at the end of the year. You may need to make estimated tax payments, and you may need to pay self-employment tax. While it's unlikely that you'll set up as a corporation, if you do, you'll need to file a corporate tax return. If you set up as a partnership, you'll need to file a partnership return. And just to make things a little more confusing, if you set up as a limited liability corporation (LLC), you might still be taxed as a sole proprietorship or partnership. Early on, you'll need to speak a tax accountant so that you have everything set up correctly. This is all easy to do if you set it up correctly from the beginning. If you get and follow good advice, and if you keep the right kind of records, taxes will be super easy. If you don't, they will be a monster headache, and you could get yourself into some real trouble.

Of course, you could always get a job as a travel agent. Host Agency Reviews cited a report from Bureau Labor Statistics (BLS) saying the "average wage of a travel agent is $18.14.hr or $37,730 annually." (hostagencyreviews.com/how-much-do-travel-agents-make-travel-agent-salary/)

Other benefits

Being an independent travel agent is fun, especially if you like traveling. You take pleasure in looking for great flights and hotels for your clients because you are not just doing this for the money, but also because you enjoy it. You can work from home—nothing beats a 10-second commute! Having your own website gives you the tools to track sales and visitors, and watch your business grow.

Drawbacks

There are some downsides of being an independent travel agent. To begin with, the income is not consistent. Most people can and do book travel on their own, and even if they book through your site, the commissions are minimal. You will probably need to put in the time to develop a local clientele in order to make a reasonable income through service fees you charge to your local customers.

As a third-party, independent travel agent, you should be free from all liability for any problems that may occur. If anything that goes wrong with the flights or the travel products, you refer your customer to the travel wholesaler to resolve the issue.

Please note that I cannot give legal advice, and you should consult a good business attorney to determine the extent of any liability exposure you may have, and to determine whether it would be advisable to purchase some type of business liability insurance.

As far as I know, it is not necessary to put disclaimer language on your travel website since you are not the main agent or the main source of the booking. Your site, if set up like mine, is just linking the customers to the travel wholesaler where they book their tickets and/or purchase their products. Again, consult an attorney as your situation may be different.

"What if I don't like it; how do I get out?"

You can shut down your independent travel agency any time you want. You'll just need to follow through on any commitments you've made to any of your customers. (The bottom line in business is this: If you make a promise, you need to keep it.) Otherwise, there are no long-term contracts to sign, or no requirements for you to stay in business for any length of time. You will not incur any financial penalties for shutting your business down. Simply remove your website, and explain to any new prospects who call you in response to your local advertising that you're no longer in the travel business. (It would be helpful if you can refer them to another trustworthy travel agent.)

Summary

Being an independent travel agent can be both fun and financially rewarding. Through affiliate marketing, you can connect your customers to travel wholesalers who provide airline tickets, hotel bookings, car rental, cruises, and travel products. While it is possible to create a passive online income through affiliate commissions and Google AdSense, you'll probably make a better income by charging service fees to local customers you serve.

Resources for further study

Scope and growth of the travel industry:

- iata.org/pressroom/pr/Pages/2013-12-30-01.aspx
- ustravel.org/answersheet

Some legal requirements for travel agents:

- travellaw.com/page/travel-law-faq

Start up costs:

- hometravelagency.com/startup-costs

Domain registrars and/or hosting companies

- godaddy.com
- pairdomains.com
- hostgator.com
- webhostinghub.com

Affiliate services:

- rakutenmarketing.com/affiliate.html
- travelerrr.com
- travelpayouts.com

Google AdSense

- google.com/adsense/start/
- nutsandboltsmedia.com/how-does-adsense-work

My travel site:

- Stopnfly.com

A great book on naming your business or website:

- bit.ly/POPname1

Earning potential:

- giftedtravelnetwork.com/ much-travel-agents-get-paid/
- hostagencyreviews.com/how-much-do-travel-agents-make-travel-agent-salary/

Free mentoring for business start up:

- score.org

Notes

Section Three: Micro-entrepreneurship Income

Lyft Driving

"The key word for transportation in the 21st is 'choice.'" ~Anthony Foxx (brainyquote.com)

Introduction

As a teacher, I have the summers off, so I became a Lyft driver in the summer of 2014. I was curious to see how this ride sharing system worked. I've enjoyed it. Every week I get money deposited into my account just for driving people around.

"Demand for ride sharing has been growing like crazy, and it shows no signs of slowing down...We talked to Paul Pruce, who's been driving full-time with Lyft for over a year. He earns $750 a week as a driver. Best of all, he does it on his own time. You can work days, nights or weekends—it's up to you!" ("Try driving with Lyft!" The Penny Hoarder, October 19, 2017, thepennyhoarder.com)

Of course, Lyft is one of several ride sharing companies. I'm not saying it's better or worse than Uber or any of the others, but my experience is with Lyft, so I'll focus on that company.

According to the Los Angeles Times, as of 2016, "Lyft has 315,000 drivers. Uber has more than 400,000 in the U.S. alone." (Tracey Lien, "Lyft defies predictions by continuing to grow as a rival to Uber," Los Angeles Times, January 5, 2016, latimes.com/business/technology/la-fi-0105-lyft-growth-20160105-story.html)

Skills, training, or licensing needed

To be eligible to be a Lyft driver, you must:

- be at least 21 years old,
- own a recent model four-door car (specific requirements vary by state),
- complete a vehicle inspection,
- have in-state insurance with your name on the policy,
- have an in-state United States driver's license,
- have one full year of United States driving experience,
- have in-state plates with a current registration (commercial plates are acceptable)

- pass a background check and a driving record check
- own a current smartphone
- comply with any local regulations in your area

(ridesharingdriver.com/lyft-driver-requirements-meaning/)

How to start (process, time, cost)

Other than the cost of owning, operating, and insuring your car, it doesn't cost anything to drive with Lyft. There is an application process. You apply at the Lyft site. (lyft.com/drive-with-lyft) You will need to provide your social security number. Applications are processed in three to ten days. Once you're approved, you provide bank information so you can be paid, or you can sign up for Express Pay (explained below).

How to get customers

As with many other ride share companies, Lyft finds your customers for you. When you activate the Lyft app on your phone, you are matched with riders as they become available in your area.

How to operate

You choose your own hours. You only drive when you choose to drive.

The Lyft website gives detailed instructions on how to provide this service:

> Before you start, open the Lyft Driver app and tap 'Go Online.' This lets you receive ride requests. To see what this looks like in the app, skip to How rides appear in the app.
>
> Once you're online, follow these steps:
>
> When you get a ride request, you'll see a notification. Tap anywhere to accept.
>
> Tap the arrow next to the pickup location
>
> Select 'Tap to arrive' when you're at the pickup location. Tap 'Confirm arrival' to send the rider a text (if we haven't already).
>
> Tap 'Pick up (passenger's name)' when the rider gets in to start the ride
>
> Tap 'Navigate' to begin navigation, then drive the rider to their destination
>
> Tap 'Tap to drop off' when you arrive at the dropoff location, then tap 'Confirm drop off' to end the ride
>
> Rate your passenger after the ride. That's it!
>
> Heads up: Passengers can tip either in the app or with cash, but don't accept money for ride fare. Passengers should use the app to pay for rides. ...
>
> You have 15 seconds to accept a ride. If you don't accept in this time, we'll offer the ride to another driver.
>
> Change your navigation preferences to automatically switch between driving mode and the map. ...

If you don't want to wait longer for your passenger, tap 'No-show.' You can choose whether to charge the passenger a no-show fee.

Pro-tip: Line passengers have 60 seconds to show, but all other ride types, including scheduled rides, have 5 minutes.

Pro-tip: Always ask the rider's name to verify it's their ride when they get in your vehicle

If the rider didn't provide a dropoff location when requesting the ride, enter one before leaving.

Don't type addresses while driving.

Some riders have preferred routes. Feel free to let them call the shots!

Tapping cancel after 'Tap to drop off' keeps you in the ride. Tapping 'Confirm drop off' ends the ride.

Ratings with 3 stars or below mean won't be matched with this passenger again. Passengers don't see passenger feedback, only Lyft.

(help.lyft.com/hc/en-us/articles/214219657-How-to-give-a-Lyft-ride)

Earning potential

"With Lyft, drivers can get paid in two ways: a weekly deposit into their checking account or Express Pay, which puts their pay on a debit card whenever they want after reaching at least $50 in ride earnings, referrals, and mentor payments. (Note: There's a 50-cent transfer fee to collect Express Pay.)" (blog.-lyft.com/posts/get-paid-quickly-express-pay)

As a Lyft driver, you are paid as an independent contractor (not an employee). You are paid by the ride, not by the hour.

According to one source, "Lyft drivers earned an average of about $17.50 per hour, or almost $2 per hour more than what was reported by Uber drivers." ("Lyft Driver: Do You Make More Money Driving for Uber or Lyft?" July 11, 2017, time.com/money/4849359/lyft-uber-driver-who-makes-more-money/)

"Most drivers are compensated at least $15-$20 whether they actually give a ride or not. So you could potentially be sitting at your house making $20 an hour 'driving' for Lyber." ["Lyber" is Harry Campbell's term for Lyft, Uber, and other ride sharing companies.] (Harry Campbell, "Have You Thought About Becoming a Driver for Lyft/Uber?" February 3, 2014, yourpfpro.com/thought-becoming-driver-lyftuber/)

You also earn bonuses for referring friends to Lyft (riders or drivers). When the new driver is signing up, s/he enters the code Lyft gives to you. Once the new driver completes a certain number of rides, you receive referral fees. It is possible to earn hundreds of dollars in referral fees, but restrictions apply. Details are at the Lyft website. (lyft.com/terms/referrals)

More on earnings can be found at the Lyft website. (help.lyft.com/hc/en-us/categories/201235657-Earnings-and-Promos)

Other benefits

If you enjoy driving and enjoy meeting new people, Lyft is a no brainer. You pick your own hours, and work as many or as few hours as you like. There's tremendous freedom, and you have complete control over your schedule.

If you're looking for a way to earn some quick extra cash, you've found it. You don't need to go searching for customers, because Lyft is doing that for you. While it might not be a high paying full-time job, it certainly can be a great income supplement.

When I first started, I signed up for both Uber and Lyft. I found Lyft to be more flexible compared to Uber. For example, with Uber if you miss two pickups they can temporarily block you from accessing the app. Also, Lyft provided a higher level of service. They sent someone to coach me on how to operate and how to maximize my revenue driving for them.

Drawbacks

"Unfortunately, driving for Uber/Lyft isn't as rosy as it sounds. Although it might vary from company to location to situation, expect a commission of around 20% to come right off the top of any fare you earn. Still, 80% isn't bad considering you're just showing up and driving people from A to B. One of the bigger costs that I'd point out is the maintenance, upkeep, gas and insurance on your car. Uber/Lyft passes along a fare to you, and that's it. You are responsible for keeping your car running. That means that all the gas, maintenance and upkeep costs will come as an expense out of the fare. So after taking out the 20% commission, you'll also have to subtract the gas costs, oil changes and repairs. Insurance companies will also be interested to know that you're now using your personal vehicle for commercial reasons, which likely will come with higher rates. Of course you could opt to skip telling them that, but you'd probably be in a lot of trouble if something goes wrong! Also, don't forget about the hidden cost of time; your phone won't be beeping with rides all the time and there will likely be some down time waiting for rides." ("The Pros and Hidden Cons of Driving for Uber/Lyft," March 15, 2017, youngmoneyfinance.com/2017/ 03/15/the-pros-and-hidden-cons-of-driving-for-uberlyft/)

You'll want to do your own research on insurance coverage. With some policies, your auto insurance coverage switches off when you turn on the ride share app. Lyft and other companies do provide insurance to cover you, but there may be a gray area of whether you're covered when the app is on, but no rider is in the car. In addition, the coverage provided by your auto insurance company may be different than the coverage provided by Lyft.

Having said that, it looks like these gaps in coverage are beginning to be filled. One source reports: "As Uber and Lyft have grown in popularity, auto insurance companies have expanded their efforts to meet the demand from drivers for coverage. Typically, rideshare insurance covers personal use and adds coverage for at least part of the time that drivers are signed in to a ridesharing app." ("Rideshare Insurance for Drivers: Where to Buy, What It Covers," August 7, 2017, nerdwallet.com/blog/insurance/best-ridesharing-insurance/)

There is an attempt by Lyft and other ride share companies to protect the public from drivers who have a criminal background. A background check is part of the application process. In some states, laws prevent certain criminals, such as registered sex offenders from driving for Lyft. I am aware, however, of no such screening for riders. However, passengers and drivers are rated by one another, and riders are not shown the ratings they receive from their drivers, so if you have a bad experience with a rider, the app protects you from being matched with that rider again. See lyft.com/safety for more information.

"What if I don't like it; how do I get out?"

You can walk away from Lyft at any time, unless, of course, you're in the middle of providing a ride for someone. All you need to do is turn the app off. Then you're done.

Summary

If you like driving, Lyft is a great opportunity to earn quick extra cash. The app matches you with people who are looking for rides, so you don't need to worry about finding customers. While some people drive for Lyft full time, most just drive in their spare time to supplement their income. Hourly earnings average $17.50 and referral bonuses are available. You need to meet requirements, and you are responsible for keeping your own car maintained and insured.

Resources for further study

Demand for ride sharing and scope of industry:

- thepennyhoarder.com
- latimes.com/business/technology/la-fi-0105-lyft-growth-20160105-story.html

Requirements:

- ridesharingdriver.com/lyft-driver-requirements-meaning/

Where to apply with Lyft:

- lyft.com/drive-with-lyft

How to give provide the service:

- help.lyft.com/hc/en-us/articles/214219657-How-to-give-a-Lyft-ride

Express pay:

- blog.lyft.com/posts/get-paid-quickly-express-pay

Earnings:

- time.com/money/4849359/lyft-uber-driver-who-makes-more-money/
- yourpfpro.com/thought-becoming-driver-lyftuber/
- lyft.com/terms/referrals
- help.lyft.com/hc/en-us/categories/201235657-Earnings-and-Promos

Drawbacks:

- youngmoneyfinance.com/2017/ 03/15/the-pros-and-hidden-cons-of-driving-for-uberlyft/

Insurance:

- nerdwallet.com/blog/insurance/best-ridesharing-insurance/

Safety:

- lyft.com/safety

Free mentoring for business start up:

- score.org

Tax Preparation

"The hardest thing in the world to understand is income taxes." ~Albert Einstein *(quoteinvestigator.com)*

Introduction

I became a tax preparer in 2011 at the request of my cousin from New York who introduced me to veteran tax preparer Yvon Jean. Jean took the time to teach me everything regarding tax preparation. Prior to meeting Jean, I thought tax preparation was too complicated. But with the training I received, I was able to quickly learn the process, to build a clientele, and establish a good side income.

There's a huge market for tax preparers. The IRS reports, "After CY 2012, the grand total return filings are projected to grow at an average annual rate of 1 percent and are expected to reach 253.5 million returns by 2018." (Brett Collins, "Projections of Federal Tax Return Filings: Calendar Years 2011–2018," irs.-gov/pub/irs-soi/12rswinbulreturnfilings.pdf) It's no surprise that there are up to 1.2 million tax preparers in the United States. (bls.gov/oes/current/oes132082.htm)

Skills, training, or licensing needed

To be a professional tax preparer, you must be at least 18 years old and have a high school diploma. In addition, you will need certain skills, training, and a Preparer Tax Identification Number from the IRS. Although the IRS does not require tax preparers to have a degree to prepare tax, you need to be informed and educated about the tax law. You need to know how to communicate with your clients to explain everything clearly. When your clients discover that you are knowledgeable, they feel comfortable to trust you to prepare their taxes.

Skills: To be an effective tax preparer, you will need:

- customer service skills
- communication skills
- math skills
- computer skills
- an ability to learn tax regulations

Training: Although you are not legally required to obtain training,[2] it's in your best interests to do so. To provide the best service for your clients and to protect yourself from liability, it's best to obtain training before you start, and update your training each year as tax laws frequently change.

---

2   Prior to the court decision from the D.C. Circuit Court of Appeals in 2013, continuing education for tax preparers was mandatory. After that decision according to accountancy.com, "the IRS had no legal authority to impose a nationwide licensing scheme on tax return preparers that would have required testing and continuing education as Registered Tax Return Preparers." (accountingtoday.com/news/tax-preparers-defeat-irs-in-appeals-court-ruling-on-licensing-scheme)

Licensing: If you prepare someone else's return and charge money for doing so, you will need at PTIN (Preparer Tax Identification Number) from the IRS which used to cost $50 per year. However, starting with the 2017 tax season, the PTIN issued by the IRS to all tax preparers is now free.

Registration and/or licensing in your state may or may not be a requirement. You'll need to research that online, or contact your state's department of revenue.

How to start (process, time, cost)

You will need to begin by obtaining your PTIN (Preparer Tax Identification Number) from the Internal Revenue Service (IRS). You obtain your PTIN at the IRS website.

(rpr.irs.gov/datamart/mainMenuUSIRS.do) Having a PTIN is the initial step to begin a tax preparation business. It is imperative to have it if you want to be compensated for the tax service you render to a customer. Without the PTIN, the IRS will impose a penalty[3] on you. The cost of the PTIN was $50 per year (becomeataxpreparer.net/obtaining_ a_PTIN.htm) but is now free.

Second, to be an effective tax preparer, you need to have training on tax preparation. Besides the guidance from my cousin Doucharde and my mentor Yvon Jean, I obtained training online on federal and state tax from TaxTalk.com. I spend $250 per year for tax refresher courses. Initial training will probably cost you about $500.

Third, I bought basic office supplies—paper, printer ink, folders, calculator, and, of course, a computer and scanner—whatever I needed to serve my clients for tax season. Since I'm working from home, nobody else is buying those supplies for me. I spent about $500 on office supplies.

Since we file our returns electronically (e-file), I needed (and you will probably need) a working Internet service.

You will probably need professional tax preparation software. Many options are available; expect to spend around $500, although cheaper—and much more expensive—options are available. Software designed for consumers is not adequate for your needs. In my case, I am working in partnership with Coulisse Community Center located in Brooklyn, New York, so I use the software they own. Coulisse owns the software. I work at home. Coulisse installs the software into my desktop.

---

3   Revenue Code (IRC) § 6695 penalties, an injunction, and/or disciplinary action by the IRS Office of Professional Responsibility

You may want to consider working for an established tax preparation firm for your first year or two as they often provide free training, allow you to use their software, and will take care of getting your customers for you while you learn the business.

If you want to become an independent contractor who owns the software to e-file taxes for your clients, you will need to obtain an EFIN (Electronic Filing Identification Number) from the IRS. There is a screening process, and you will need to submit a set of fingerprints. More information is available at the IRS site. (irs.gov/e-file-providers/become-an-authorized-e-file-provider)

How to get customers

I find my clients through referrals from friends and colleagues. In addition, I print business cards and fliers to advertise my tax preparation service. My very first clients were friends and family members. Progressively, I started to build my clientele through referrals. Using these methods, I've attracted clients from New Jersey, New York, Pennsylvania, Massachusetts, Wisconsin, and Florida. I only prepare individual income tax returns as opposed to corporate or partnership returns.

If a client does not accept our conditions for the tax to be done legally and ethically, then that persons is welcome to go somewhere else. Entrepreneur Chris Guillebeau wrote: "For your micro-business, the best way to generate value for your customers is by making their lives better in some ways, instead of just focusing on making money for yourself." (Chris Gillebeau, *The $100 Startup: Reinvent the Way You Make a Living, Do*

What You Love, and Create a New Future, 2016, hoopladigital.com/play/11661480) As a professional tax preparer, I maintain a high standard and serve my clients according to the tax law.

How to operate

Since I started being a tax preparer in 2011, I have been working with Coulisse Community Center of Brooklyn, NY under the leadership of Yvon Jean. That partnership has been been helpful for me because I have a mentor who has helped me get established in the business, and I have someone I can turn to if I have questions.

Since the tax laws change every year, it is important to stay informed and updated about the new rules and regulations that affect your clients.

Tax preparation is a seasonal business; you only work from January to April each year to serve your clients. You can work as many hours as your client load requires, and as you have capacity to work. Since I work full time as a teacher, I'm only available part time to help clients with their taxes.

Although the bulk of your training will be around preparing federal income tax returns, your professional tax software will guide you in the preparation of state (and, in some cases, local) income tax returns.

Earning potential

As a part time tax seasonal tax preparer, I make a good side income every year. On average, I bring in an extra $5,000 each year, although that amount varies from year to year.

Since I work from home, I don't get the walk-in traffic that I might get if I had an office in a busy strip mall, for example. Since I have a full-time teaching job, my income as a tax preparer is limited by the hours I have available—generally only evenings and weekends.

According to Glassdoor.com, "The national average part-time tax preparer salary is $26,557." However, recruiter.com adds "Tax Preparers can make the most money in Massachusetts, which has average pay levels of approximately $60,440." It's not clear whether those numbers refer to self-employed tax preparers, or those who are employed by tax preparation firms, or both.

Other benefits

If you enjoy math, learning, and working with people, this is a fun way to earn extra money. Push hard for four months, and you'll have extra money for the rest of the year. Remember that your expenses are deductible.

This is a very secure business. Benjamin Franklin said, "In this world nothing can be said to be certain, except death and taxes." What was true in the 1700s is even more true today. There will always be people who need help with their taxes. Learn your craft, provide good service, and you can be virtually assured of having a steady stream of clients each tax season.

The only way to get kicked out of this business is for the IRS to revoke your credentials as a tax preparer, and if you're trustworthy and conscientious, that's not going to happen.

Drawbacks

Tax preparation is a seasonal business. You cannot rely on it for a steady income year round. For some people who have the flexibility, that's not a problem. For others, you'll need to develop other income supplements to sustain you from May to December.

The amount of money you will make is somewhat unpredictable. Every season will be different.

Competition. Since there are so many tax preparers out there, you need to set yourself apart by focusing in on a niche, by becoming extremely knowledgeable, or by acquiring some other advantage that sets you apart from your competition.

Every tax season is different in terms of revenue. Since there are many tax preparers out there you have to set yourself apart to be educated about the federal and state tax laws to better serve your clients with professionalism.

Liability. What happens if you make a mistake preparing someone's taxes? For example, what happens if you under-report someone's income? If you were negligent, you could be liable. According to *Marquette Law Review*, "Because of the contractual relationship, the practitioner may be liable to the taxpayer, his client, for negligence resulting in damages. If there is an understatement of tax on the original return which later results in a deficiency upon audit, the practitioner may be liable, because of his negligence, for additional interest on the deficiency." (Louis L. Meldman, "The Legal Responsibilities of the Person Preparing Tax Returns and Furnishing Tax Advice and Reliance Upon Advice of Counsel," *Marquette Law Review*, Volume 46 Issue 3 Winter 1962-1963.)

Errors and omissions insurance is available for tax preparers. If you are interested, the annual premium usually runs somewhere between $350 and $700. (financial.insureon.com/resources/cost/tax-preparers)

"What if I don't like it; how do I get out?"

Suppose you become a tax preparer and decide it's not for you. How hard is it to leave the business? Not hard at all. You merely need to keep the commitments you've already made to your clients, and then step away. There are no long-term contracts to tie you down. It's easy to step away.

Summary

If you enjoy learning, math, and working with clients, becoming a tax preparer is a great way to make supplemental income. It is a seasonal business, so you'll work many hours from January to April, but then you'll have the rest of the year to enjoy the extra income you make during that time.

Resources for further study

Scope and growth of tax preparation industry:

- irs.gov/pub/irs-soi/12rswinbulreturnfilings.pdf
- bls.gov/oes/current/oes132082.htm

Training requirements:

- accountingtoday.com/news/tax-preparers-defeat-irs-in-appeals-court-ruling-on-licensing-scheme

Obtaining your PTIN/Preparer Tax Identification Number:

- rpr.irs.gov/datamart/mainMenuUSIRS.dobecomeataxpreparer.net/obtaining_ a_PTIN.htm

Online tax training:

- TaxTalk.com
- cpaacademy.org

Obtaining an EFIN/Electronic Filing Identification Number:

- irs.gov/e-file-providers/become-an-authorized-e-file-provider

Becoming an entrepreneur:

- Chris Gillebeau, *The $100 Startup: Reinvent the Way You Make a Living, Do What You Love, and Create a New Future*, 2016, hoopladigital.com/play/11661480

Free mentoring for business start up:

- score.org

Earning potential:

- Glassdoor.com
- recruiter.com

Errors and omissions insurance

- financial.insureon.com/resources/cost/tax-preparers

Liability information:

- Louis L. Meldman, "The Legal Responsibilities of the Person Preparing Tax Returns and Furnishing Tax Advice and Reliance Upon Advice of Counsel," *Marquette Law Review*, Volume 46 Issue 3 Winter 1962-1963.

ESL Instruction

"To have another language is to possess a second soul." ~Charlemagne (brainyquote.com)

Introduction

Since 2015 I have been supplementing my income teaching English as a Second Language (ESL) part time at the UCEDA School in Elizabeth, New Jersey. (ucedaschool.edu/) This is a private school, and you don't need to be a certified teacher to provide ESL instruction. (I am a World Language certified full-time high school teacher with a master's degree, but I am not certified in ESL instruction per se.) Most of the time, I am on call as a substitute teacher when the regular ESL instructor is absent.

People from non-English-speaking countries come to the United States for many different reasons including education, political asylum, business, employment, family. All of these people need to speak and write the English language in order to function properly in the American society and culture. This creates a huge demand for ESL instruction.

"According to a U.S. Census Bureau report, 55.4 million people in the United States reported speaking a different non-English language at home, making ESL teachers a necessity in today's schools. The teacher shortage is not only due to the rapid growth in population, but also the changing demographic of those students. As many as 10.5 percent of students in the United States do not speak English as their first language. California and Texas are the top two states in which non-English children are more likely to require the services of a teacher with ESL certification or TESOL certification. Illinois, Florida and New York also have high concentrations of immigrants." (Cathryn Vandewater, "The Growing Demand for ESL Teachers: ESL Teacher Shortage Areas," December 04, 2013 certificationmap.com/the-growing-demand-for-esl-teachers-esl-teacher-shortage-areas/).

In addition, many persons for whom English is a second language seek out private instruction from individuals or from private schools where ESL teaching certification is not required.

If you have the skills and patience to help immigrant adults to master the English language, the opportunities are wide open for you.

Skills, training, or licensing needed

To teach English as a Second Language in a public high school requires an ESL teaching certification issued by the state's department of public instruction (or equivalent).

However, requirements can be more flexible in a business school, private institute, evening school, college extension, or other settings which are not (as a rule) funded by tax dollars. Generally speaking you will need:

- a college degree,
- some experience teaching adults,

- patience.

While not required, it is helpful if you speak your students' first language, at least a little. For example, if you speak a little Spanish while teaching English to Hispanic immigrants, students from the basic level will be more comfortable interacting with you and you will find it easier to communicate.

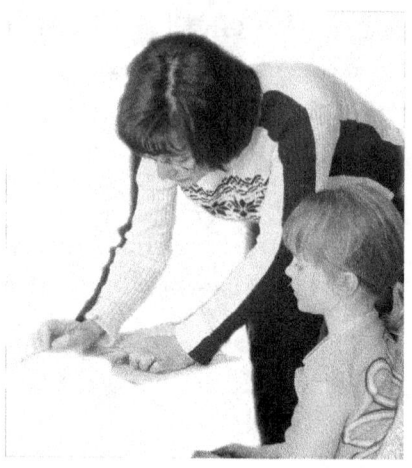

How to start (process, time, cost)

I obtained my part-time position by applying with the UCEDA School. (ucedaschool.edu/career-opportunities/) A similar process may be available for teaching at other private schools. In addition, on the job training may be available. For example, at the UCEDA School, the school coordinator provides training for new ESL instructors.

On the other hand, you could set up shop as a freelance ESL instructor. You'll have control over your schedule and fees, and could potentially work almost anywhere in the world. But you'll need to find your own students, your income will be unpredictable, and you'll need to do your homework to make sure you follow legal requirements for the area in which you are working. (Bernard, "How to Start Your Freelance ESL Teaching Career," July 20, 2016, blog.invoiceberry.com/2016/07/how-to-start-freelance-esl-teaching/)

How to get customers

Instead of opening my own school where it would take time to develop a reputation and attract students, I chose to work with a well established franchise in an area of the country where there is a large immigrant population with a desire to learn English. That way, I don't need to be concerned about finding students.

If you are planning to freelance, one source gives this advice: "In order to grow your business, remember to get your customers through various means, such as advertising in advance, in-class advertising, or paper marketing; set competitive rates that reflect your experience—remember to do your research first, then find the level at which students are willing to pay for your services; build your reputation through being a good teacher, and then start going to events to network yourself." (blog.invoiceberry.com/2016/07/how-to-start-freelance-esl-teaching/)

How to operate

The private institute where I teach ESL is well organized. The school has a morning, evening and weekend schedules in order to accommodate students with different schedules. They provide instructors with English textbooks and learning CDs. Students buy their books at the school. Each class lasts for two hours. Students practice English speaking, writing, listening, and grammar every day. Before they move to the next level, students take an exam in order to measure their proficiency.

If you are interested in teaching ESL abroad, be aware that this can be both rewarding and very demanding. Many countries, particularly Asian countries like Japan, China and South Korea need ESL teachers for their elementary, middle and high school children. However, a deep commitment and plenty of patience is required to teach foreigners in a foreign country where you do not know much about their culture.

Earning potential

The institute where I teach pays me $16 per hour.

The average cost for an ESL Tutor ranges from $30 to $40 per hour. (thumbtack.com/p/esl-prices)

Other benefits

It can be immensely satisfying helping others adjust to a new language, a new culture, a new set of experiences. If you enjoy teaching, have patience, and respect others who have a different set of life experiences, you will find ESL instruction rewarding.

Drawbacks

If you travel abroad to do ESL instruction, be sure to do your homework. Not all agencies that employ ESL instructors are following the legal requirements of the country in which they are working. This could result in you being arrested and/or deported. (Zoe Leavitt and Aaron Lee, "How English Teachers in China Are Lied to and Exploited," Jan 28 2015, vice.com/en_us/article/av4pvj/the-chinese-esl-industrial-complex-shady-working-conditions-abound-for-foreign-english-teachers-in-china-127)

"What if I don't like it; how do I get out?"

As with any business or job, you need to keep your promises. If you've agreed to teach a certain class or student for a certain term, you need to honor those commitments. Beyond that, if you choose not to renew your contract, that's up to you. Typically, you won't have a large (or any) financial investment to worry about, so you'll be walking away without losing any money other than potential earnings.

Summary

If you have a bachelor's degree, experience teaching adults, and some proficiency with language, then becoming an ESL instructor can be a rewarding experience. It's easiest and safest to work with an established ESL franchise with a good reputation in order to avoid some of the pitfalls that can be associated with this line of work. While many ESL instructors do work full time, part time opportunities are also available.

Resources for further study

Demand for ESL instruction:

- certificationmap.com/the-growing-demand-for-esl-teachers-esl-teacher-shortage-areas/

Opportunties with the UCEDA School:

- ucedaschool.edu/career-opportunities/

How to start a freelance ESL teaching career:

- blog.invoiceberry.com/2016/07/how-to-start-freelance-esl-teaching/

Earning potential:

- thumbtack.com/p/esl-prices

Dangers of working for an agency that fails to follow legal requirements:

- vice.com/en_us/article/av4pvj/the-chinese-esl-industrial-complex-shady-working-conditions-abound-for-foreign-english-teachers-in-china-127

Free mentoring for business start up:

- score.org

ATM Deployment

"Folks can't carry around money in their pocket. They've got to go to an ATM machine, and they've got to pay a few dollars to get their own dollars out of the machine. Who ever thought you'd pay cash to get cash? That's where we've gotten to." ~Bill Janklow (brainyquote.com)

Introduction

As an entrepreneur, in my quest to find side income to bolster my savings, I discovered that you can own your own money machine. Prior to that discovery, I thought all ATM machines at grocery stores, malls, airports, restaurants, gas stations, train stations, and so on were owned by a big bank. In reality, 48% of ATM machines in the United States are owned by financial institutions while 52% are owned by independent operators. (statisticbrain.com/atm-machine-statistics/)

This is a huge market. "There's 370,000 automated teller machines across the United States right now, about 1 for every 296 people." (Bob Sullivan, "Are there too many ATMs?" nbcnews.com/id/5529813/ns/business-personal_finance/t/are-there-too-many-atms/#.WXGfhCMrKu4)

Another source puts the number of ATM machines in the United States at 425,000 and the total number in the world at 3,000,000. (statisticbrain.com/atm-machine-statistics/)

Consider these ATM machine statistics

- Average number of transactions per ATM machine per month: 800

- Average ATM withdrawal amount: $60

- Average increase in sales for a store that installs an ATM machine: 20 %

- Percent of money dispensed at bars and clubs that is spent there: 75 %

- Percent increase in spending of an ATM user over a non-ATM user: 23 %

- Average number of times a person visits an ATM machine per month: 7.4

- Number of new ATM machines installed each day in the world: 280

Source: statisticbrain.com/atm-machine-statistics/

According to an ATM machine buyer's guide, "3%–5% of the foot traffic that actually sees the ATM machine will use the ATM." (atmexperts.com/atm_machine_buyers_guide.html)

If your ATM machine is processing 800 transactions per month, and you earn $2 per transaction, that $1,600 in your pocket. And the only work you really need to do is replenish the cash and the paper in the receipt printer. Owning an ATM machine cannot only produce a side income; it is a business by itself that can generate a great income.

My Side Income: 7 ways to put more money in your pocket

Skills, training, or licensing needed

The skills required for operating an ATM business are not that complex. You'll need to be flexible enough to respond to any issues that come up with the machine (paper jams, out of cash, etc.)

Your ATM vendor will train you on how to fix the machine, how to change the printer paper, how to clear a paper jam, and how to replenish cash in the vault. You become proficient at those things because you do them over and over again. When a problem occurs, you can handle it. You won't need to pay a technician to clear a paper jam for you. You can do it yourself and save the money that you might have otherwise spent on a service call.

In New Jersey, you are not required to have a business license to buy an ATM machine. The requirement may be different in other states. In addition, there may be local licensing considerations, so be sure to check with your local municipality.

As a sole proprietor, you run your business independently. If you decide to buy a franchise or be an ATM wholesaler, you may need additional licensing, or you may need to comply with additional ordinances and/or pay added local taxes.

How to start (process, time, cost)

I contacted an ATM distributor in New York to learn about the process of buying an ATM machine. The distributor explained everything to me in terms of sales, installation, profitability, marketing, and so on.

First things first: Before you buy your ATM machine, you need to secure a location where it is going to be placed. If you want to make a great side income from your ATM machine, location is key. For the security of your customers and for your own security when replenishing the cash in your machine, the area should be under 24 hour video surveillance and there should be a mirror so customers can see the person behind them in line when they are using the machine.

You need traffic, and lots of it. By traffic I mean how many people each day frequent the location where you plan to locate your ATM machine. Location is crucial for your ATM business to flourish. Remember, you are in the business to make money.

Do the math. If you want your ATM machine to generate $1,000 in revenue each month, that means you'll need 500 transactions each month. That's 17 transactions per day, seven days a week. If 3% of the foot traffic that sees your ATM machine each day will use it, that means that you want over 550 people walking past that ATM machine each day. Of course, your odds should improve once customers get accustomed to using your ATM machine and start making it part of their regular routine. According to statisticbrain.com, the "average number of times a person visits an ATM per month is 7.4" More and more people are visiting ATM machines than ever before. And there's no reason to think that trend won't continue.

I secured a location in a take-out restaurant in New Jersey. The owner of the store was happy to have the ATM installed at his facility because customers were always asking for an ATM in order for them to get money to pay for their groceries. The store owner did NOT charge me any rent. Here's why: Not only was I helping this restaurant owner provide a valuable service to his customers, having an ATM machine at his location was drawing more customers to his store. He is making more money because my machine is there.

In some cases, the owner of a location may charge you a fee for using the space. You'll need to decide if the cost is worth it, or if you would be better off looking for a different location.

Once I obtained permission from the owner of the location where I wanted to place my ATM machine, I ordered the machine from a company distributor in New York. My ATM machine cost me less than $3000. I had it installed in November 2013, and it has been making money for me at that location ever since.

How much does it cost to buy an ATM machine? The price of buying a machine can be between $2,000 and $10,000. It depends on the model of the machine and accessories you want to add on. Leasing an ATM machine is an option that may make sense for some people. If you lease, you don't need to come up with the funds to purchase the ATM machine, and the leasing company might take care of some maintenance needs. However, that low monthly leasing payment often means you'll end up paying quite a bit more in the long run. Read the lease carefully and show it to your accountant. For some people there are tax advantages to leasing. For others, you're far better off buying your ATM machine outright.

The ATM machine I purchased typically has a trouble-free life of about seven years. You'll need to research the useful life of the ATM machine you choose to purchase. Once the useful life is up, you'll want to think about updating your machine.

I supplied the cash to fund the ATM machine. I started with just $200 in cash, although I've since learned that it's good to keep at least $1,000 in cash in the machine. (Otherwise, you'll be constantly returning to the machine to restock the cash.) In any case, I considered it an investment. When a customer makes a withdrawal from my machine, a processor deposits those fund (plus my fee) into my account the next day. These deposits provide funds for replacement cash.

That particular brand of ATM machine I purchased allows me to print advertising on the receipt and on the screen. Three local businesses advertise in my machine. This provides a source of revenue in addition to the transaction fees.

How to get customers

Location! Location! Location! Since your customers are coming to you, you need to be where the people are. Your customers will use your ATM machine if (1) they are walking past it, and (2) if they need/want to pay cash for some kind of purchase nearby. That's why a grocery store or shopping mall is a perfect place for an ATM machine.

How to operate

Once your ATM machine is up and running, you need to be concerned with three things:

1. Cash. You need to keep your machine stocked with cash. I have an app on my phone supplied by the ATM machine distributor that lets me know when my machine is running low on cash.

While I supplied the cash to fund the machine at the beginning, the processor deposits money in my account each day to cover the withdrawals from the previous day plus my fees. So the money for the replacement cash is already waiting for me in my account.

You have a choice between restocking the machine yourself or hiring armed security to load the cash into your ATM machine. ATMDepot.com suggests, "There are two factors to take into consideration when deciding who will stock your ATM: safety and convenience." I try to take in both of these factors into consideration, and I choose to replenish the cash myself. Not only is it far less expensive, but I'm operating in a place of high visibility with video monitoring so my risks are low. I try my best not to replenish cash during peak times so I don't inconvenience customers.

I suggest you don't advertise the fact that you own an ATM machine, and especially don't spread the word that you stock it with cash yourself. You don't want this information in the hands of the wrong person. Why make yourself a target?

2. Paper. The paper in the receipt printer needs to be replaced regularly. In addition, I occasionally need to clear paper jams inside the machine. Paper in the receipt printer can last for months depending on the usage. And there's no way to predict how often you'll have paper jams, but it doesn't happen very often.

3. Maintenance and repair. While your ATM machine should be mostly trouble free, if issues come up, your ATM machine distributor or your payments processor should be able to help you find the right technician or other resource to take care of any repairs.

Be sure to budget something for machine replacement. ATM machines, like any other business equipment, don't last forever.

If you buy a used ATM machine to start your business, make sure you verify if the EMV (Europay, MasterCard, and Visa) is installed into it. If not, you must buy it in order to comply with the new regulations. If you don't have it, you expose yourself to liability. According to Lend Genius, "Basically what this means is that if a customer comes in a charges $1000 on an EMV chip card, and you use the old magnetic card swiper to ring them up, that customer can dispute the charge and you as the EMV non-compliant merchant would have no legal recourse." (LendGenius.com) If you don't want to pay a penalty as an ATM deployer, you need the EMV card reader in your machine. In addition, it is a good tool to prevent credit card fraud.

Earning potential

The ATM business can produce a great side income if you have a good location that has a lot of traffic.

The more ATM machines you have at various locations, the more money you could make. According to CNN, the average fee for an out-of-network ATM withdrawal in 2016 was $4.57. (money.cnn.com/2016/10/04/pf/atm-record-fees/) Do the math: $4.57 times 1,000 transactions is $4,570 in your pocket. That's not out of reach, especially if you have several machines in good locations.

In addition to the fees you charge for each transaction, you will also receive a small amount of revenue if the form of an interchange fee. What is interchange fee? "Interchange fees are transaction fees that the merchant's bank account must pay whenever a customer uses a credit/debit card to make a purchase from their store. The fees are paid to the card-issuing bank to cover handling costs, fraud and bad debt costs and the risk involved in approving the payment." (bigcommerce.com)

It took two and half years for my ATM machine to pay for itself. Ever since, all the money I make in transaction fees is pure profit—except for the negligible cost of maintenance and supplies (e.g., paper for printer). How soon you recover your investment depends on a number of factors; the most important one is the location of your ATM machine.

Having said all of that, you cannot predict exactly how much you will earn each month. Your earnings are based on the laws of averages. Some months your earnings might spike while in other months they may dip. Circumstances beyond your control may affect your earnings. For example, if the business where you have located your machine closes or moves to a different location, you may be scrambling to find a different place to put your machine.

Other benefits

As with any business, your business expenses are deductible. You'll need to talk with your accountant to determine whether the cost of your ATM machine can be expensed the same year you purchase it, or whether you'll need to depreciate it over time.

Your ATM machine can be connected to an app on your phone making it easy to track any problems or whether you need to replenish the cash in the machine.

While this isn't exactly a "wind it up and forget it" investment, it is a business that requires only a minimal amount of time each day. Your machine is making money for you; you don't need to be present for that to happen.

Drawbacks

Like any other business, owning an ATM machine has its downsides. You do need to respond quickly to any needs with the machine. If it's out of cash, you need to refill it right away. If the receipt printer out of paper, you need to replace the paper right away. So it's not as though you can wind it up and forget about it. You do need to take care of it.

More importantly, if you place your ATM machine in a bad location, you will have problems. If few people frequent the location, then you'll find yourself losing money rather than making money.

Two years after I bought my first ATM machine, I bought a second machine from a company in New Jersey. I placed in a pizzeria in New Jersey. Unfortunately, the business closed the year after. While that was happening, my machine was smashed with a hammer because the place was vandalized. I ended up selling the parts to the distributor in New Jersey.

If someone robs the business where your machine is placed, your machine can be at risk for damage and vandalism. This is a concern. "Some of the threats and challenges you are likely to face when starting your ATM business are; thefts, online frauds, network connectivity issues and changes in technological trends." (profitableventure.com/starting-an-atm-business/)

What about security? What happens if someone breaks open your ATM machine? I've placed my ATM machine in a take-out restaurant where there are active security cameras inside. You also have the option to take out insurance on your ATM machine and its contents in case something should happen.

Some people are concerned about ATM skimmers. ATM skimmers are devices designed to steal a customer's debit card information for the purpose of committing fraud. They are sometimes attached to ATM machines in an attempt to harvest financial data from customers. So far, no one has ever tried to place an ATM skimmer on my ATM machine.

Obviously, ATM machines rely on technology, and technology is subject to glitches. But, so far, I haven't run into any problems. My ATM machine has never, for example, dispensed the wrong amount of money.

No-fee ATMs. Even though some financial institutions offer their customers free ATM transactions, people still visit my ATM machine and pay the fees. Most people would prefer the convenience of cash in hand right now to driving across town to visit their no-fee ATM.

Insurance. As an independent ATM agent you are free to purchase insurance for your machine. Insurance is not mandatory. You may want to carry insurance to protect your asset especially if your ATM machine is located in an area with high risk for potential vandalism. If your machine is damaged, the insurance will reimburse you for your loss. According to ATMdepot.com, insurance may be a waste of money if your location is open 24 hours a day and/or has good alarms and security cameras.

"What if I don't like it; how do I get out?"

If you decide that owning an ATM machine is not for you, the easiest way out is to sell your machine to another agent. That way you recoup at least some of your investment.

Summary

Owning an ATM machine can be a lucrative side business that requires a minimal time commitment for the amount of money that you earn. But you do need to be flexible and responsive to keep your ATM machine fully stocked and functioning for your customers. Your return on investment should be far more than you would earn just putting your money in the bank and hoping to earn a little interest. The key with this business is to place your ATM machine in a good location.

As an entrepreneur, ATM deployment is lucrative business that can generate a lot of of Benjamins for you every month if you have several machines in good locations.

Resources for further study

Scope and growth of the ATM industry:

- statisticbrain.com/atm-machine-statistics/
- Bob Sullivan, "Are there too many ATMs?" nbcnews.com/id/5529813/ns/business-personal_finance/t/are-there-too-many-atms/#.WXGfhCMrKu4
- atmexperts.com/atm_machine_buyers_guide.html

Best practices:

- ATMDepot.com
- LendGenius.com

Earning potential:

- money.cnn.com/2016/10/04/pf/atm-record-fees/

Interchange fees:

- bigcommerce.com

Risks:

- profitableventure.com/starting-an-atm-business/
- ATMdepot.com

Free mentoring for business start up:

- score.org

Notes

Section Four: Passive Income

Investment

"How many millionaires do you know who have become wealthy by investing in savings accounts? I rest my case." ~Robert G. Allen (investopedia.com)

Introduction

Money doesn't grown on trees. You need to earn it. We all know this. But what do you do with that money? You can't put it under a mattress. Once you've earned it—how do you make it grow?

I quickly discovered that banks do not make you rich. On the contrary, by depositing your money in a savings or checking account, you enrich the bank instead. In our current economy, getting 1% annual interest from a bank is about the best you can expect. Most of the time, the return is far below 1%.

Looking at that grim reality forced me to explore another option: investing. I discovered that I can invest a little money month after month to make my earnings grow.

Skills, training, or licensing needed

Anyone can invest, but, because investing carries a certain level of risk, you want to do your homework before you sink your hard earned money into investments. That means you'll want to read what you can and talk to other investors. A Google search on "best books on investing" will connect you with a wealth of information. In some localities, there are investment groups you can join. Some groups pool their knowledge and their money, and invest together. Others simply share knowledge, and individuals choose their own investments. In any case, you'll want to get advice from friends, family, colleagues, experienced investors. You may even want to pay a financial planner to guide you.

How to start (process, time, cost)

Investopedia offers this advice, "Once you've determined the shape of your portfolio, it is time to invest. Find a broker you are comfortable with, either an online broker or one with a local office or both. Call and talk with this person if necessary. Then fill out the paperwork, deposit some money and open an account." (investopedia.com/articles/basics/07/getting-started-stocks.asp) Fees for online trading are usually about $5 to $7 per trade. Some online brokerage firms also charge a monthly service fee. Nerd Wallet offers a list of online brokers for investors who are just starting out. (nerdwallet.com/blog/investing/the-best-online-brokers-for-beginners/) Some brokerage firms offer tools to help investors, so the benefit of these tools needs to be weighed against any fees charged.

How to find investments

Which investments are right for you? That depends on many factors—how much money you have to invest, whether you're looking for growth or income (or both), your tolerance for risk, how long you want to hold each investment, the amount of time you have to spend on investing, and so on. Because the goals and needs of each investor are unique to that individual, I am NOT to give you advice on which investments to choose. You need to make that decision yourself based on the best advice you can obtain. But I will share with you which investments I chose and why.

You need to understand that "past performance is not indicative of future results." In other words, just because a stock did well in the past does not mean it will do well in the future. And vice versa. This is why you want to invest with your eyes wide open, paying attention to all the trends and other factors that might affect how your investments will perform.

In my case, I did my research online. I read what other investors had to say about the pros and cons of different stocks and other investments. Before investing in a company, I wanted to know how the company performed in the market over a long term period.

After doing my research, I chose to invest in Southwest Airlines, Lending Club, and Realty Income Corporation. Let me tell you about each of those investments.

Southwest Airlines is one of the major airlines in the United States and the world's largest low-cost carrier. I identified this stock while browsing on the website of Shareowner Online, a financial service manage by Wells Fargo. I found Shareowner Online convenient because I did not need to go to a brokerage office to purchase stocks. From the comfort of my home I could browse through many investments on their website and choose which ones to purchase from there. More information on Shareowner Online here: goo.gl/PmiDsU

I found that I could invest in Southwest with as little as $250, and gradually increase my portfolio from there. Each quarter, I receive dividends directly deposited into my checking account.

I also invested in Lending Club. I chose Lending Club because the lending market is doing well. According to CNN Money, "Americans had $3.843 trillion in loans outstanding in May, up from $3.766 trillion at the end of last year, according to the Fed." (money.cnn.com/2017/08/07/investing/trump-economy-report-card/index.html)

Lending Club is a peer-to-peer lending company located in California. What is a peer to peer lending? According to SelectCore Ltd., "Peer-to-peer lending, sometimes abbreviated P2P lending, is the practice of lending money to individuals or businesses through online services that match lenders with borrowers." (goo.gl/yckhQ6). Lending Club, an online service between lenders and borrowers, allows people to invest their money and in return to receive a monthly dividends.

According to their website, "Lending Club is America's largest marketplace connecting borrowers and investors, where consumers and small business owners lower the cost of their credit and enjoy a better experience than traditional bank lending, and investors earn attractive risk-adjusted returns.

"Here's how it works:

- "Customers interested in a loan complete a simple application at LendingClub.com

- "We leverage online data and technology to quickly assess risk, determine a credit rating and assign appropriate interest rates. Qualified applicants receive offers in just minutes and can evaluate loan options with no impact to their credit score

- "Investors ranging from individuals to institutions select loans in which to invest and can earn monthly returns

"The entire process is online, using technology to lower the cost of credit and pass the savings back in the form of lower rates for borrowers and solid returns for investors."

(lendingclub.com/public/how-peer-lending-works.action)

As an investor, I just invest my money. Lending Club deals with the borrowers. Each month, I receive returns deposited in my checking account.

I also have invested in Realty Income Corporation, a real estate investment trust that invests in shopping centers in the United States and Puerto Rico. In their portfolio, they have more than 5,028 commercial properties. Among them are Walmart/Sam's Clubs, Walgreens, BJ's, etc. Their real estate assets are up to $14.4 billion. (realtyincome.com)

I buy shares in this company because they pay monthly cash dividends to the shareholders. They have a proven record of keeping their tenants for a long term lease agreements. Long-term leases lower the risk, making it easier for the company to pay out monthly dividends.

As an investor in Realty Income Corporation, I am NOT directly involved in the day-to-day operations of this company. I don't purchase sites, hire contractors, negotiate leases, collect rents, make repairs, and so on. In other words, I don't personally invest directly in real estate. But many investors do, and many have built their wealth by investing in rental properties and/or real estate development projects. Here a deep knowledge of your investment is required. This type of real estate investing tends to be much more hands on. Although the rewards can be great, the risks are real, and a substantial initial investment is often required.

Annuities. Any discussion of investments would not be complete without mentioning annuities. An annuity is "a contractual financial product sold by financial institutions that is designed to accept and grow funds from an individual and then, upon annuitization, pay out a stream of payments to the individual at a later point in time." (investopia.com) In other words, a financial institution will manage your annuity investment over a period of time when you were actively working, and then will send you a stream of payments when you reach a certain age. There are penalties for withdrawing funds prior to reaching age 59½.

There are three types of annuities:

1. Fixed Annuities act like a savings account.
2. Variable Annuities act more like a mutual fund.
3. Equity Indexed Annuities act like a hybrid of fixed annuities and variable annuities.

(Jeff Rose, "Is an Annuity the Worst Investment a Young Person Can Make?" Good Financial Cents, July 27, 2017, goodfinancialcents.com/should-you-buy-annuity/)

Are annuities right for you? It depends. Jeff Rose recommends that you fully fund your Roth IRA and your 401K before investing in an annuity.

Payments (payroll deductions or direct payments) into your annuity are tax deferred until withdrawn at or around retirement age. (But you will pay a 10% penalty if you withdraw early.)

In some cases, Other advantage I find out is that the annuity in many cases is exempt from creditors. According to Money Crashers, "Annuity contracts are also largely exempt from creditors in many cases, although the exact rules for this vary somewhat from one state to another. Texas is one state that unconditionally exempts these contracts from creditors; O.J. Simpson lived on money he had in annuities after the civil judgment against him in 1994 (but before his more recent incarceration)." (Mark Cussen, "What Is an Annuity and How Does It Work? – Annuities Explained," Money Crashers, moneycrashers.com/what-is-annuity-how-does-it-work-annuities-explained/) Check your state banking department to see if your annuity is exempt from creditors.

I invest in an annuity because it provides (1) steady interest even the market goes down, (2) tax deferred payment, (3) steady payments once I reach age 59½, (4) protection from creditors (protection varies by state).

Your financial adviser and/or the benefits counselor from your human resources department should be able to tell you how to invest in an annuity. Get good advice because if your annuity is not set up properly, your payments into it will not be tax deferred.

Another type of investment

While it makes a great deal of sense to invest in stocks and other securities, don't neglect investing in yourself. Markets change. Economies collapse. Your wealth can be wiped out in a day. But what you put in your mind is there to stay.

Paul Clitheroe wrote, "Invest in yourself. Your career is the engine of your wealth." (investopia.com)

Invest time and money to learn skills that will allow you to survive and thrive no matter what. Some skills, like sales, marketing, negotiation, and business development will be helpful to you no matter what you do. Other, more specialized skills may be in demand, and may open doors of opportunity for you. Suppose you become proficient in Mandarin Chinese, or C#, or cost accounting. What opportunities could these skills create for you?

In this era of technology, you don't even need to set foot in a classroom if you don't want to. Many traditional schools are offering inexpensive online course. In addition, non-traditional schools or e-learning platforms like Udemy and Udacity offer courses where you pay a small fee and learn at your own pace.

"Udemy is a global marketplace for learning and teaching online where students are mastering new skills and achieving their goals by learning from an extensive library of over 65,000 courses taught by expert instructors." (about.udemy.com/)

"Udacity [udacity.com] is a for-profit educational organization founded by Sebastian Thrun, David Stavens, and Mike Sokolsky offering massive open online courses (MOOCs). According to Thrun, the origin of the name Udacity comes from the company's desire to be 'audacious for you, the student.'" (Wikipedia)

Benjamin Franklin put it well when he said, "An investment in knowledge pays the best interest."

How to operate

You can take two approaches to investment: investing or trading. According to Investopedia, "Investing and trading are two very different methods of attempting to profit in the financial markets. The goal of investing is to gradually build wealth over an extended period of time through the buying and holding of a portfolio of stocks, baskets of stocks, mutual funds, bonds and other investment instruments. Investors often enhance their profits through compounding, or reinvesting any profits and dividends into additional shares of stock. Investments are often held for a period of years, or even decades, taking advantage of perks like interest, dividends and stock splits along the way. While markets inevitably fluctuate, investors will 'ride out' the downtrends with the expectation that prices will rebound and any losses will eventually be recovered. Investors are typically more concerned with market fundamentals, such as price/earnings ratios and management forecasts.

"Trading, on the other hand, involves the more frequent buying and selling of stock, commodities, currency pairs or other instruments, with the goal of generating returns that outperform buy-and-hold investing. While investors may be content with a 10 to 15% annual return, traders might seek a 10% return each month. Trading profits are generated through buying at a lower price and selling at a higher price within a relatively short period of time. The reverse is also true: trading profits are made by selling at a higher price and buying to cover at a lower price (known as 'selling short') to profit in falling markets. Where buy-and-hold investors wait out less profitable positions, traders must make profits (or take losses) within a specified period of time, and often use a protective stop loss order to automatically close out losing positions at a predetermined price level. Traders often employ technical analysis tools, such as moving averages and stochastic oscillators, to find high-probability trading setups."

("What is the difference between investing and trading?" Investopedia, investopedia.com/ask/answers/12/difference-investing-trading.asp)

Earning potential

Earning 5% to 20% (or more) annually on your investment is certainly possible, but not guaranteed. You might lose money. You might lose your entire investment. So it's impossible to predict how much money you will earn, but there are certain things you can do to improve the odds for you. Matthew Frankel recommends these four guidelines:

"1. Don't try to time the market. Buying a stock or fund because you think it's at the bottom, or selling one because you think it has topped out, is almost always a losing battle. Investors who decided to buy Radio Shack after it dropped below $1 per share, or who sold Amazon.com the first time it surpassed $300, can tell you that. Instead of focusing on the share price, buy stocks that represent a business you'd like to own for the next 10, 20, or 30 years. Or, if you're a mutual fund investor, invest in quality funds regardless of what the market is doing.

"2. Don't chase hot stocks. Chasing stocks on their way up is too much of a gamble. Sure, a stock that has quadrupled in value over the past year could continue on its upward trajectory —or it could come crashing down as soon as anything goes wrong.

"3. Don't panic during crashes. Panic-selling is the worst investment move you can make during tough times. Those investors who sold out of fear in late 2008 simply turned paper losses into real losses, and they also missed the rally that took place over the next several years.

"4. Use the power of dollar-cost averaging. Dollar-cost averaging is a strategy that involves investing equal dollar amounts at regular time intervals (say, $500 every other month). Not only does this take emotion out of the equation, but it actually gives you a long-term mathematical advantage, since you buy more shares when prices are low and fewer shares when prices are high."

(Matthew Frankel, "The Average American's Investment Returns—and How You Can Do Better" The Motley Fool, Nov 1, 2015, fool.com/investing/general/2015/11/01/the-average-americans-investment-returns-and-how-y.aspx)

Other benefits

Passive income (the income associated with most investments) can offer certain tax advantages not available with earned income. For example, I don't need to pay self-employment tax on passive income.

When you own stock in a company, you are a shareholder the same way Warren Buffet may be a shareholder through his company, Berkshire Hathaway. Your shares have the same standing as the shares of a billionaire. You earn dividends and capital gains just like anyone else.

Drawbacks

Risk. Any investments that you make carries an element of risk. As my aunt said in French "qui ne risque rien n'a rien" (nothing ventured nothing gained). In other words, if you don't try something, you will never gain anything. For example, if you invest in Lending Club as I do, and if a borrower is delinquent or misses payment to the loan, then you as investor you will not receive a dividend in your account that month. According to their website, "Lending Club Notes are not guaranteed or insured and investors may have negative returns. Borrowers make payments on their loans to Lending Club and Lending Club passes those payments on to investors net of fees. If borrowers miss a loan payment, you will not receive a monthly payment on the corresponding Note. Lending Club uses best practices from the banking industry to collect payments from delinquent borrowers, but it is inevitable that some borrowers will default on their loan." (lendingclub.com)

In addition to risks associated with specific investments, there are risks connected to the market and to the economy as a whole. Market volatility is real. The stock market goes up, and the stock market goes down. If the stock market crashes and you need to cash in your investment, you could experience substantial losses.

"What if I don't like it; how do I get out?"

Some investments, such as annuities have a substantial penalty for early withdrawal. Some investments, such as rental real estate, need to be sold—a process which could take months or even years. Other investments, such as most stocks, can be liquidated at any time. Of course, it's often unwise to sell a stock simply because of a dip in the market. Smart investors ride out the storm if at all possible. As you plan your investments, your exit strategy will be part of the consideration that will govern which investments are best for you.

Summary

Earning extra money is great. Making that money grow is even better. In today's economy, your money won't earn an acceptable return in a savings account. Other investment vehicles are needed. Each investment carries certain risks and certain rewards. Which investments are best for you depends on many variables, so you'll want to do your research, and get good advice. But many believe the stock market will continue to be a good investment. As Investopedia puts it, "Based on the actions of many investors, it appears that there is still a strong belief that participating in the U.S. stock market will bring about valuable gains." (investopedia.com/ask/answers/06/usstockmarketandeconomy.asp)

Resources for further study

Best books on investing

- Beverly Bird, "The 9 Best Books on Investing to Buy in 2018," The Balance, updated January 12, 2018, thebalance.com/best-books-about-investing-4155082

- Marvin Dumon, "Top 5 Books Every Young Investor Must Read," Investopedia, updated December 29, 2017, investopedia.com/articles/younginvestors/09/5-books-for-investors.asp

- time.com/money/collection-post/3926814/best-investing-books-shiller-malkiel/

Getting started:

- investopedia.com/articles/basics/07/getting-started-stocks.asp)

Online brokerage firms for new investors:

- nerdwallet.com/blog/investing/the-best-online-brokers-for-beginners/

Shareowner Online:

- goo.gl/PmiDsU

Investment and credit climate:

- money.cnn.com/2017/08/07/investing/trump-economy-report-card/index.html

Peer-to-peer lending explained:

- goo.gl/yckhQ6
- lendingclub.com/public/how-peer-lending-works.action

Realty Income Corporation:

- realtyincome.com

Annuities:

- Jeff Rose, "Is an Annuity the Worst Investment a Young Person Can Make?" Good Financial Cents, July 27, 2017, goodfinancialcents.com/should-you-buy-annuity/
- Mark Cussen, "What Is an Annuity and How Does It Work? – Annuities Explained," Money Crashers, mon-

eycrashers.com/what-is-annuity-how-does-it-work-annuities-explained/

Online learning centers:

- about.udemy.com/
- udacity.com

Investing vs. trading:

- "What is the difference between investing and trading?" Investopedia, investopedia.com/ask/answers/12/difference-investing-trading.asp

Earning potential

- Matthew Frankel, "The Average American's Investment Returns—and How You Can Do Better" The Motley Fool, Nov 1, 2015, fool.com/investing/general/2015/ 11/01/the-average-americans-investment-returns-and-how-y.aspx
- investopedia.com/ask/answers/06/usstockmarketandeconomy.asp

Notes

Conclusion

Supplementing and growing your income will help you build a better life. Here are six reasons I recommend you put into practice the things you've learned in this book:

1. Extra income empowers you to pay those extra, unexpected bills.

2. Extra income allows you to build wealth.

3. Extra income puts you on the path to financial security.

4. Earning extra income allows you to develop your entrepreneurial skills.

5. Extra income allows you to get out of debt faster. Why waste money on all those interest payments?

6. The financial security that comes with extra income will diminish anxiety, stress, and insomnia. It will allow you to refocus your energy on something productive.

Acknowledgments

This book would not have been possible without the input, assistance, and encouragement of many individuals. I am especially indebted to Mr. Yvan Maxi, CEO of Optimum Financial services for his encouragement and advice. I wish to thank friends like Jimmy Gabriel and Joe Brutus for their generosity. I am grateful for my sister Edeline, my pastor and colleague Donatien, and others who have supported me, read the manuscript, and pushed me to the finish line in order to reach the millions of readers who would benefit from *My Side Income*. I am also indebted to Ms. Tammy Jones, English teacher, who patiently proof read the entire manuscript..

www.ingramcontent.com/pod-product-compliance
Lightning Source LLC
Chambersburg PA
CBHW071212220526
45468CB00002B/573